OLD YELLOWSTONE VIEWS

OLD
YELLOWSTONE
VIEWS

John F. Barber

MOUNTAIN PRESS PUBLISHING COMPANY
Missoula

Libraryof Congress Cataloging in Publication Data

Barber, John F.
  Old Yellowstone Views.

  Bibliography: p.91
  1. Yellowstone National Park—History. 2. Yellowstone
National Park—Pictorial works. I. Title.
F722.B24   1987   978.7'52   87—5791
ISBN   0-87842-212-9 (pbk.)

MOUNTAIN PRESS PUBLISHING COMPANY
Missoula, Montana 59806

CONTENTS

INTRODUCTION

FROM THE EARLY nineteenth century to around 1936, from the first recorded visits to the advent of mass visitation in motorized touring cars, Yellowstone National Park has spawned a rich history and many interesting stories. This history and the accompanying stories are best told by people who visited Yellowstone during this time period, people who actually participated in the events described.

Many of these Yellowstone visitors wrote their thoughts, feelings, and impressions in letters, diaries, and journals. Using cameras, they recorded photographic views of what they saw in Yellowstone.

Old Yellowstone Views is a personalized, richly illustrated oral and visual history of Yellowstone National Park told in the words and pictures of early Yellowstone visitors. It is a collection of their thoughts, feelings, and impressions.

Together, the words and pictures of these Yellowstone visitors make our sense of history more vivid and near at hand. These words and pictures, these old Yellowstone views, make us present in the past and provide an interesting account of Yellowstone's early history.

YELLOWSTONE'S FIRST VISITORS

IN THE BEGINNING Yellowstone was just another part of the seemingly interminable expanse of wilderness stretching across the continent. The land, the mountains, and the wanderings of the rivers were all unknown.

The first visitors to present-day Yellowstone National Park probably were prehistoric, nomadic people who hunted and foraged along Yellowstone's rivers and streams at least 11,000 years ago. Other than a few projectile points, they left no records of their visits.

After them came other Stone Age people who, as evidence suggests, developed into aboriginal groupings and eventually evolved into the Indian tribes of modern times.

By the early nineteenth century, these Indian tribes were firmly settled around Yellowstone. The Blackfoot lived generally to the north, the Shoshone to the west and south, and the Crow to the east.

The Crow considered the Yellowstone region their homeland and spoke eloquently of its attributes:

The Crow country...is a good country. The Great Spirit has put it exactly in the right place; while you are in it you fare well; whenever you go out of it, whichever way you travel, you fare worse.

Arapooish
Crow Chief

Along with the Crow, Blackfoot, and Shoshone, the Bannock, Flathead, and Nez Perce Indians also visited Yellowstone
trips to the buffalo ranges in eastern Montana and Wyoming.

Although these Indians visited Yellowstone, only a small band of Shoshones lived here year-round. They were called "Sheepeaters" because the mountain sheep was a staple of their diet.

The Sheepeaters did not have horses or guns like other Indians and could not compete effectively in Indian society. They found sanctuary and little competition in Yellowstone. They lived here until 1871 when they joined other Shoshones on the Wind River Indian Reservation at Fort Washakie, Wyoming.

In 1803, Yellowstone was included in the Louisiana Purchase when the United States bought from France the territory extending west from the Mississippi River to the Rocky Mountains and north and south between the Canadian and Mexican borders.

To many Americans, this addition to the country meant new opportunities. They thought the Louisiana Purchase should be explored, the wilderness subdued, the land developed, and the Indians "civilized."

The unknown areas west of the Mississippi River, including Yellowstone, called out to those brave enough to go there.

For a transitory enchanted moment man must have held his breath in the presence of this continent.

F. Scott Fitzgerald

In 1805, Meriwether Lewis and William Clark followed the Missouri and Columbia River systems across the unknown expanse of the Louisiana Purchase on their way to the Pacific Ocean. Anxious to explore the area south of the Missouri River during their return to St. Louis in 1806, Clark, a small group of men, and the famous Indian woman, Sacajawea, followed the Yellowstone River to its confluence with the Missouri.

Although they passed within sixty miles, Clark and his group did not visit Yellowstone. A member of the expedition, John Colter, did, however, and is generally considered to be Yellowstone's first Caucasian visitor.

4

John Colter was a hunter for the Lewis and Clark Expedition. On the return trip, closer to home than he had been in a year and a half, Colter met Forrest Hancock and Joseph Dixon, two fur trappers bound for the middle reaches of the Yellowstone River. They persuaded Colter to join them.

Colter asked Captains Lewis and Clark to release him from service so he could return to the mountains. They agreed and discharged him on August 5, 1806, at the Mandan Indian villages on the Missouri River; and, as Sgt. John Ordway, next in command to Lewis and Clark, wrote in his journal, they

> *Settled with him and fitted him out with powder and lead and a great number of articles which completed him for a trapping voiage* [sic] *of two years.*

Colter trapped and explored in the Yellowstone region with Hancock and Dixon during the winter of 1806. The following spring he again tried returning to civilization. But he met Manuel Lisa who persuaded him to return to the mountains once again, this time in the employ of the Missouri Fur Trading Company.

Lisa built a fort at the confluence of the Bighorn and Yellowstone Rivers. He intended this fort to become a trading center for Indians.

Lisa sent Colter out into the surrounding wilderness with instructions to find Indians and persuade them to trade at the new fort. While on this mission in the winter of 1807, Colter probably visited what is now Yellowstone National Park.

Following Colter's lead, fur trappers explored and visited Yellowstone. They were a special breed, these fur trappers.

[Each] *had his own horses and accoutrements, arms and ammunition. He took what route he thought fit, hunted and trapped when and where he chose; traded with the Indians; sold his furs to whoever offered highest for them; dressed flauntingly, and generally had an Indian wife and half-breed children. They prided themselves on their hardihood and courage... Each claimed to own the best horse; to have had the wildest adventures; to have made the most narrow escapes; to have killed the greatest number of bears and Indians; to be the greatest favorite with the Indian belles, the greatest consumer of alcohol, and to have the most money to spend... Oftener than any other way he was some wild youth who, after an escapade in the society of his native place, sought safety from reproach or punishment in the wilderness. Or he was some disappointed man who, with feelings embittered towards his fellows, preferred the seclusion of the forest and mountain. Many were a class disreputable everywhere, who gladly embraced a life not subject to social laws. A few were brave, independent, and hardy spirits, who delighted in the hardships and the wild adventures their calling made necessary. All these men, the best with the worst, were subject to no will but their own... Even their lives, and those of their companions, when it depended upon their own prudence, were but lightly considered.*

Frances Fuller Victor, 1870

By 1830, Yellowstone was well known to fur trappers. Several had their impressions of Yellowstone published in books and magazines of the day.

Warren Angus Ferris visited Yellowstone to see thermal features described to him by fellow fur trappers. He wrote this about his visit:

I had heard in the summer of 1833, while at rendezvous, that remarkable boiling springs had been discovered on the sources of the Madison, by a party of trappers, in their spring hunt; of which the accounts they gave, were so very astonishing, that I determined to examine them myself... Having now an opportunity of paying them a visit, and as another or a better might not occur, I parted with the company after supper, and taking with me two Pend d'Orielles (who were induced to take the excursion with me by the promise of an extra present), set out at a round pace, the night being clear and comfortable. We proceeded over the plain about twenty miles, and halted until daylight, on a fine spring, flowing into Camas Creek. Refreshed by a few hours sleep, we started again after a hasty breakfast... and rode about forty miles; which was a hard day's ride, taking into consideration the rough irregularity of the country through which we traveled.

We regaled ourselves with a cup of coffee, the materials for making which we had brought with us, and immediately after supper, lay down to rest, sleepy and much fatigued. The continual roar of the springs, however, (which was distinctly heard) for some time prevented my going to sleep.

When I arose in the morning, clouds of vapor seemed like a dense fog to overhang the springs, from which frequent reports or explosions of different loudness, constantly assailed our ears...

From the surface of a rocky plain or table burst forth columns of water of various dimensions, projecting high in the air, accompanied by loud explosions and sulphurous vapors, which were highly disagreeable to the smell... The largest of these beautiful fountains projects a column of boiling water several feet in diameter to the height of more than one hundred and fifty feet... accompanied with a tremendous noise. These explosions and discharges occur at intervals of about two hours. After having witnessed three of them, I ventured near enough to put my hand into the waters of its basin, but withdrew it instantly, for the heat of the water in this immense cauldron was altogether too great for my comfort... and the hollow unearthly rumbling under the rock on which I stood, so ill accorded with my notions of personal safety, that I retreated back precipitately to a respectable distance.

Warren Angus Ferris, 1834

Although Yellowstone was thoroughly tracked and explored by fur trappers, it was not officially "discovered" until 1869.

In September of that year, David E. Folsom, Charles W. Cook, and William Peterson ascended the Yellowstone River past its confluence with the Gardner River and explored Tower Fall, the Yellowstone Canyon and its falls, the Yellowstone Lake area, the Lower Geyser Basin, and the Midway Geyser Basin.

Their accounts of what they saw interested another group of would-be Yellowstone explorers. On August 22, 1870, Nathaniel Pit Langford, General Henry Washburn, Cornelius Hedges, and Lt. Gustavus Cheyney Doane embarked on an unofficial survey of Yellowstone following a route similar to the earlier Folsom-Cook-Peterson expedition.

Langford, Washburn, Hedges, and Doane wondered how they could benefit from their Yellowstone findings. According to Langford, a novel idea developed during a campfire discussion:

Tuesday, September 20, 1870... Last night, and also this morning in camp, the entire party had a rather unusual discussion. The proposition was made by some members that we utilize the result of our exploration...for the benefit of the entire party.

Mr. Hedges then said that he did not approve of any of these plans – that there ought to be no private ownership of any portion of that region, but that the whole of it ought to be set apart as a great National Park, and that each one of us ought to make an effort to have this accomplished. His suggestion met with an instantaneous and favorable response from all – except one – of the members of our party, and each hour since the matter was first broached, our enthusiasm has increased. It has been the main theme of our conversation to-day as we journeyed. I lay awake half of last night thinking about it...

Nathaniel P. Langford

Upon their return to civilization, members of the Langford-Washburn-Hedges-Doane expedition began an extensive writing and lobbying campaign promoting the idea of preserving Yellowstone as a national park. Langford made a speaking tour of several eastern cities. Doane's official report was accepted and printed by Congress.

*Self portrait of
William Henry Jackson,
Yellowstone's
first photographer.*

All this publicity resulted in congressional appropriations for The Sundry Civil Bill of March 3, 1871, authorizing the exploration of Yellowstone by the Geological Survey of the Territories headed by Dr. Ferdinand Vandiveer Hayden.

Hayden knew that to prove the existence of Yellowstone's wonders he would need documented evidence. Photographs, he felt, would be just the thing. And a young photographer, working for the western railroads, attracted his attention as the person to make them.

Hayden asked William Henry Jackson to serve as his expedition's official photographer. Jackson eagerly accepted. Thus began the first organized, government expedition to visit Yellowstone.

8

William Henry Jackson and The Hayden Survey

The First Photographs and The First Official Expedition

WILLIAM HENRY JACKSON was twenty-eight years old in June of 1871 when he joined the Hayden Survey party to explore a remote region in the northwest corner of the Wyoming Territory known as Yellowstone. Accounts of Yellowstone's steaming earth and boiling water had circulated since the early 1800s. Hayden and Jackson would prove or disprove these legends.

Born in Keesville, New York, in 1843, Jackson showed artistic talent at an early age. At eighteen he worked as a photographer's artist in Rutland, Vermont, retouching and coloring portraits. Here he learned the mechanics and skills of photography.

After service in the Civil War, Jackson returned to Burlington, Vermont, where he worked for another photographer. A quarrel with his fiancée sent him traveling out West on sheer impulse.

The move was a good one. After a stint as a cowpuncher and horse wrangler, Jackson went to work for a photographer in Omaha, Nebraska. He quickly bought out his employer and, with his brother who had followed him West, went into business as "Jackson Brothers, Photographers."

Jackson's photographic equipment consisted of an 8"x10" format camera, a 6½"x8½" "miniature" camera, and a stereo camera for the production of stereopticon views. He also had a specially made portable darkroom tent, several hundred sheets of glass in various sizes to be used as photographic plates in his various cameras, and the necessary chemicals for sensitizing these plates. His gear weighed over 300 pounds and was carried by a pack mule named "Hypo."

Jackson photographed from the tops of mountains, the bottoms of canyons, and everywhere in between. Wherever the mule couldn't go, Jackson and his assistant carried the necessary gear themselves.

Once a scene was selected for photographing, one or more tripods were set up, cameras were mounted on them, and the scene was composed and focused on the ground-glass viewing screens.

Jose and Joe Clark bringing in elk meat for the Hayden Survey party, 1871.
William Henry Jackson photograph courtesy National Park Service, Yellowstone National Park.

Then the darkroom tent was erected, and the photographic plates prepared. These plates had to be exposed and developed before they dried or they lost much of their sensitivity to light. Exposure times were sometimes as long as two to three minutes.

Jackson's photographic work for the western railroads attracted Dr. Hayden's attention and prompted the invitation to join the Yellowstone expedition.

Members of the Hayden Survey party met and established a rendezvous camp near Ogden, Utah. In addition to the technical personnel, there was a young artist named Thomas Moran who, fresh from success in Europe, found the American West worthy of the grand style, romantic imagination, and rich coloring of his master, J.M.W. Turner.

Twenty other men served as packers, cooks, laborers, hunters, and guides. After all the gear was rechecked and packed, they started the long trek to Yellowstone.

Near present-day Emigrant, Montana, the Hayden Survey party began following the Langford-Washburn-Hedges-Doane route southward along the Yellowstone River. As they approached the Yellowstone region, members of the Hayden Survey party eagerly anticipated their findings and spent much time speculating around the campfires.

After reaching the junction of the Yellowstone and Gardner Rivers, the Hayden Survey party traveled up a valley with walls of volcanic rock, "like the refuse about an old furnace" as Hayden wrote in his field journal.

Members of the Hayden Survey Party, 1872. Left to right: W. H. Holmes, artist; Unknown; W. H. Jackson, photographer; C. R. Campbell, photographer's assistant; and Dr. A. C. Peals, mineralogist. William Henry Jackson photograph courtesy National Park Service, Yellowstone National Park.

Dr. Ferdinand V. Hayden and Walter Paris in camp, 1871.
William Henry Jackson photograph courtesy National Park Service, Yellowstone National Park.

They passed the remains of several hot springs, and then

After ascending the side of the mountain, about a mile above the channel of [the] Gardner River, we suddenly came in full view of one of the finest displays of nature's architectural skill the world can provide. Before us was a hill two hundred feet high, composed of the deposit of the springs, with a system of step-like terraces which would defy any description by words.

F.V. Hayden, 1871

Hayden did find words, however, to describe these formations, and Jackson beautifully documented them with photographs.

The steep sides of the hill were ornamented with a series of semi-circular basins, with margins varying in height and so beautifully scalloped and adorned with a sort of bead-work that the beholder stands amazed. Add to this a snow-white ground, with every variety of shade in scarlet, green and yellow as brilliant as the brightest dyes.

The pools or basins are of all sizes from a few inches to six or eight feet in diameter, and from two inches to two feet deep.

F.V. Hayden, 1871

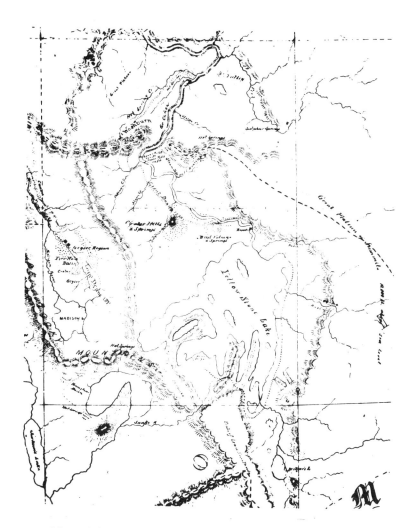

Map of the Yellowstone region prepared by Lt. Gustavus Doane, 1870.
Courtesy National Park Service,
Yellowstone National Park.

13

Mammoth Hot Springs, Upper Basin, 1871.
William Henry Jackson photograph courtesy National Park Service, Yellowstone National Park.

As we pass up to the base of the principal terrace, we find a... remarkable cone, about forty feet in height and twenty feet in diameter at the base. It is undoubtedly the remains of an extinct geyser. We gave it the name of the "Liberty Cap."

F.V. Hayden, 1871

Leaving the Mammoth Hot Springs area, the Hayden Survey party traveled east along the Yellowstone River to Tower Creek. There they saw, and Jackson photographed, Tower Fall. From Tower Fall they rode their horses to the top of Mount Washburn to gain an overview of the Yellowstone region.

The view from the summit is one of the finest I have ever seen...an area of fifty to a hundred mile radius in every direction could be seen more or less distinctly. We had a first glimpse of... [Yellowstone Lake]. To the south are the Tetons, monarchs of all they survey, their summits covered with perpetual snow. Southwest, an immense area of dense pine forests extends for one hundred miles. To the north we get a full view of the valley of the Yellowstone, with the lofty ranges that wall it in.

F.V. Hayden, 1871

But the objects of deepest interest in this region are the Grand Canyon and the Falls. As we approached the margin of the canyon, we could hear the suppressed roar of the falls, resembling distant thunder.

Standing near the margin and looking down the canyon, an immense chasm or cleft in the basalt, with its sides 1200 to 1500 feet high, and decorated with the most brilliant colors, the rocks weathered into an almost unlimited variety of forms and here and there a pine tree sending its roots into the clefts on the sides as if struggling with the uncertainty for existence, the mind of the onlooker is seized with impressions of grandeur. Mr. Moran exclaimed with a kind of regretful enthusiasm that these tints were beyond the resources of human art. The waters of the Yellowstone seem, as it were, to gather themselves into one compact mass and plunge over the descent of 350 feet in foam as white as snow. Upon the yellow, nearly vertical western side, the mist mostly falls, and for 300 feet from the bottom of the wall is covered with a thick matting of mosses, sedges, grasses, and other vegetation of the most vivid green, which have sent their small roots into the softened rocks and are nourished by the ever-ascending spray.

F.V. Hayden, 1871

15

16

Lower Falls of the
Yellowstone River, 1872.

William Henry Jackson photograph
courtesy National Park Service,
Yellowstone National Park.

Upper Falls of the
Yellowstone River, 1871.
William Henry Jackson
photograph courtesy
National Park Service,
Yellowstone National Park.

From the Grand Canyon of the Yellowstone, with its magnificent falls, Hayden led his survey party along the Yellowstone River and through a broad valley, which would later bear his name, to the shores of Yellowstone Lake.

...a vast sheet of quiet water, of a most delicate ultramarine hue, one of the most beautiful scenes I have ever beheld... Such a vision is worth a lifetime, and only one of such marvelous beauty will ever greet human eyes.

F.V. Hayden, 1871

Members of the Hayden Survey party assembled the framework for a twelve-foot boat and covered it with a "skin" of well-tarred canvas. This boat was named the *Anna*, for the daughter of Senator Henry M. Dawes of Massachusetts, who had lobbied successfully for the financing of Hayden's expedition.

James Stevenson (Hayden's assistant) and Henry Elliott sailed the *Anna* to an island which Hayden named for Stevenson, considering him to be "undoubtedly the first white man that ever placed foot upon it." Later, they used the *Anna* to measure depths around the lake.

From Yellowstone Lake the Hayden Survey party traveled to the Firehole River valley. Here they found a grand display of geysers and boiling springs. Jackson's photographs beautifully supported the accounts of these wonders told by earlier visitors.

The Castle Geyser received its name from its resemblance to the ruins of an old castle as one enters the valley from the east. The entire mound is about forty feet high, and the chimney twenty feet. This has undoubtedly been one of the most active and powerful geysers in the basin; it still keeps up a great roaring inside, and every few moments throws out a column of water to the height of ten or fifteen feet; all around it are most beautifully ornamented reservoirs that receive the surplus waters.

F. V. Hayden, 1871

The Anna, *first boat on Yellowstone Lake, 1871. The name* Annie *was mistakenly added to the photograph later.*
William Henry Jackson photograph courtesy National Park Service, Yellowstone National Park.

The Hayden Survey party enroute through the Yellowstone wilderness, 1871

William Henry Jackson photograph courtesy National Park Service, Yellowstone National Park.

18

View looking across the Firehole River valley, 1871. Crested Hot Spring is in the foreground, Old Faithful geyser is erupting in the background.

William Henry Jackson photograph courtesy National Park Service, Yellowstone National Park.

Castle Geyser, Upper Geyser Basin, 1871.

William Henry Jackson photograph courtesy National Park Service, Yellowstone National Park.

19

Old Faithful Geyser erupting, 1871. Members of the Hayden Survey party are standing nearby.

William Henry Jackson photograph courtesy National Park Service, Yellowstone National Park.

Early in the morning, as we were leaving the valley, the grand old geyser which stands sentinel at the head of the valley gave us a magnificent parting display, and with little or no preliminary warning it shot up a column of water to the height of 100 to 150 feet. By a succession of impulses, it seemed to hold the column steadily for the space of fifteen minutes, the great mass of water falling directly back into the basin and over the edges and down the sides in large streams. When the action ceases, the water recedes beyond sight and nothing is heard but the occasional escape of steam until another exhibition occurs....

This is one of the most accommodating geysers in the basin and during our stay played once an hour quite regularly. On account of its regularity and its position overlooking the valley Messrs. Langford and Doane called it "Old Faithful." It has built up a crater about 20 feet high around its base, and all about it are decorations similar to those previously described.

F.V. Hayden, 1871

After completing their explorations, the Hayden Survey party left Yellowstone with masses of notes, sketches, photographs, specimens, raw scientific data, and a sense of wonder and awe.

The Liberty Cap.
William Henry Jackson photograph
courtesy National Park Service,
Yellowstone National Park.

*Mammoth Hot
Springs, Lower
Basin, 1871.*
William Henry Jackson
photograph courtesy
National Park Service,
Yellowstone National Park.

*Hayden Survey party
camped on shore of
Yellowstone Lake, 1871.*
William Henry Jackson photograph
courtesy National Park Service,
Yellowstone National Park.

Mammoth Hot Springs, 1871.
William Henry Jackson photograph courtesy National Park Service, Yellowstone National Park.

Grand Canyon of the
Yellowstone, from brink
of Lower Falls, 1871

William Henry Jackson photograph
courtesy National Park Service,
Yellowstone National Park.

Tower Fall, 1871

William Henry Jackson photograph
courtesy National Park Service,
Yellowstone National Park.

23

Yellowstone River, from the top of Upper Falls, 1871.
William Henry Jackson photograph courtesy National Park Service, Yellowstone National Park.

Upper Firehole River valley from cone of Old Faithful Geyser, 1872.
William Henry Jackson photograph courtesy National Park Service, Yellowstone National Park.

When Hayden returned to his office in Washington, he found much interest in developing legislation to preserve the Yellowstone wilderness. This interest was enthusiastically supported by the newly-elected delegate to Congress from the Montana Territory, William H. Clagett.

Hayden, Clagett, and Langford, who continued to speak and write about preserving Yellowstone, met in Washington and laid plans for presenting the "National Park project" to Congress. They personally visited members of Congress to convince them to support the park bill. Many of the specimens the Hayden Survey party brought from Yellowstone were displayed and explained.

Meanwhile, William Henry Jackson was quietly preparing prints from his precious glass negatives. This was the trump card Hayden held for his final lobbying effort.

At just the right moment, handsomely bound folio volumes of Jackson's photographs, each neatly captioned and bearing the name of the recipient stamped in gold, were placed on the desks of all members of Congress. Those photographs helped convince a skeptical Congress that Yellowstone should be preserved.

On March 1, 1872, Congress approved an act creating Yellowstone National Park, the nation's and the world's first national park.

Be it enacted by the Senate and House of Representatives of the United States of America in Congress assembled, That the tract of land in the territories of Montana and Wyoming, lying near the headwaters of the Yellowstone River... is hereby reserved and withdrawn from settlement, occupancy, or sale under the laws of the United States, and dedicated and set apart as a public park or pleasuring ground for the benefit and enjoyment of the people...

Signed by:
James G. Blaine,
   Speaker of the House
Schuyler Colfax,
   Vice-President
   of the United States
   and President of the Senate
Ulysses S. Grant,
   President of the United States

Artist Thomas Moran climbing on the Mammoth Hot Springs terraces, 1871.
William Henry Jackson photograph courtesy National Park Service, Yellowstone National Park.

Army Days in Yellowstone

WHEN CONGRESS ESTABLISHED Yellowstone National Park in 1872, despite its good intentions, it did not provide for the park's administration or protection. Supporters of the park bill knew that the economy-minded Forty-second Congress would refuse any proposal that increased the federal expenditure. Park legislation therefore was presented as an idea that could be managed without cost to the government.

It was believed that concessionaire operations would provide for the administration and protection of the new national park. The idea was that as more people visited Yellowstone attractive business opportunities would develop for concessionaires catering to the needs of these visitors. Franchise fees collected from the concessionaires would support the park's administration and protection.

Such was not the case though. People visited Yellowstone, but they did not share or were not aware of the park's preservation policy. Yellowstone suffered under their onslaught. Fires were set, animals killed, thermal features disrupted, and natural objects destroyed. Concessionaires did little or nothing to assure the protection and preservation of Yellowstone.

During the thirty years following the designation of Yellowstone National Park, Congress appointed several superintendents and assistant superintendents to provide some direct administration of the park. Funds were sporadically approved for salaries and improvements, but in some cases administrators were forced to compromise in order to survive financially.

A monstrous headache was created for Congress as corruption, abuse, and misuse of the new national park grew to unchecked proportions. Park historian Hiram M. Chittenden summarized these problems in 1895 when he wrote:

> *The common verdict, as gathered from official reports and other sources, is that the body of police styled assistant superintendents, were notoriously inefficient, if not positively corrupt. They were, for the most part, creatures of political favoritism, and were totally unused to the service required of them. Commissioned as guardians of the rarest natural wonders on the globe, they not infrequently made merchandise of the treasures which they were appointed to preserve. Under their surveillance, vandalism was practically unchecked, and the slaughter of game carried on for private profit almost in sight of the superintendent's quarters.*

Camp Sheridan, circa 1910. The Norris Blockhouse is seen atop Capital Hill in the center.
Courtesy National Park Service, Yellowstone National Park.

The situation in Yellowstone became desperate. Something had to be done. In 1886, using an obscure law, the Secretary of the Interior called on the Secretary of War for help in protecting Yellowstone. The U.S Cavalry rode to the rescue, and for the next thirty years administered and protected Yellowstone National Park.

On August 17, 1886, Captain Moses Harris and fifty men of Company M, First United States Cavalry, of Fort Custer, Montana Territory, arrived at Mammoth Hot Springs and established a tent camp at the base of the hot spring's terraces. They called their new home Camp Sheridan in honor of Lieutenant General Phillip H. Sheridan, hero of the Civil War Battle of Cedar Run.

Captain Harris assumed the duties of Superintendent of Yellowstone National Park and immediately went to work. He stationed soldiers at various points formerly occupied by the Assistant Superintendents. Park regulations were issued and he gave his soldiers clear instructions as to their enforcement.

It is enjoined upon all soldiers, when on duty at points frequented by tourists, to be vigilant and attentive in the [enforcement of the] regulations... They will also at all times exert themselves to preserve peace and order at the points where they are stationed. They will in the enforcement of their orders conduct themselves in a courteous and polite, but firm and decided manner. They will not hesitate to make arrests when necessary...

Captain Moses Harris, 1886

Soldiers in front of the Canyon Soldier Station, 1906.
Courtesy National Park Service, Yellowstone National Park.

Ski patrol to Fall River. Ski scouts (l. to r.) Morrison, Stitham, Holte, and Lindsay.
Courtesy National Park Service, Yellowstone National Park.

Yellowstone was patrolled by soldiers to protect the wildlife from poachers.

> *...squads are sent over the Park, and instructed not to follow the regular trails, but to go to the most unfrequented places, so that they may at any time happen on a malicious person, and perhaps be able to do as one scout did – photograph the miscreant with his own camera.*

Frederic Remington, 1893

Frederic Remington was a well-established illustrator when he visited Yellowstone National Park in 1893. He was seeking subjects to portray with his paint brush and ink pen.

Protection of the wildlife continued through the winter months, and Captain Harris utilized a patrol method that overcame the difficulties of traveling through the deep snow. While in Yellowstone, Remington observed a group of soldiers on ski patrol.

> *In winter the snow covers the ground to a great depth... The rounds of the Park are then made by mounting the cavalry on the ski, or Norwegian snowshoe, and with its aid men travel the desolate snow-clad wilderness from one "shack" to another. Small squads of three or four men are quartered in these remote recesses of the savage mountains, and remain for eight months on a stretch. The camps are provisioned for arctic siege, and what is stranger yet is that soldiers rather like it, and freely apply for this detached service... They are dressed in fur caps, California blanket coats, leggings, and moccasins – a strange uniform for a cavalryman, and also quite a commentary on what are commonly called the vicissitudes of the service.*

Frederic Remington, 1893

Soldiers on ski patrol at the Grand Canyon of the Yellowstone, 1910.
Courtesy National Park Service, Yellowstone National Park.

Generally, the soldiers enjoyed their isolated duty, but there were occasional low moments. One soldier remembered them when he recounted in 1919:

> *When the winter starts to drag and the playing cards are worn to rags; when the reading matter that has done for years of service gets still older, and, as the lights in the cabin are extinguished for the night, and the coyotes assemble and yelp, that is when "old grouch" affects each man. Every morning he gets up, looks at the same faces, eats, puts on his skis, goes out for his patrol, comes back, eats, and lies down, to do the same thing the next day.*

Thomas M. Connery

With no legal machinery established by Congress, Captain Harris and his soldiers relied on the provisions within the Yellowstone Act of 1872 for protecting the park. This created some unusual methods of protection and punishment.

Owen Wister, a western writer and author of *The Virginian,* visited Yellowstone several times between the late 1800s and the early 1900s. He made this observation about the Army's protection of Yellowstone National Park in 1891:

> [The soldiers] *devised punishment for the offenders before punishment was provided by law. The soldiers patrolled the places where vandalism was likely to occur. If they caught a tourist writing on the formation or breaking it off they stopped him, compelled him to efface the writing and give up the specimen. If they found a name after its writer had gone on they rode after him and brought him back to rub it out.*

Another Yellowstone visitor who recorded his observations about the Army's handling of troublemakers was Rudyard Kipling.

When Kipling visited Yellowstone in 1889, he was twenty-four years old. He was making a leisurely trip across the United States traveling from England to India, the country of his birth. He wrote:

> [The terraces are] *guarded by soldiers who patrol it with loaded six-shooters, in order that the tourist may not bring up fence rails and sink them in a pool, or chip the fretted tracery of the formations with a geological hammer, or, walking where the crust is too thin, foolishly cook himself.*

Although not as famous as Wister or Kipling, James B. Wasden, a sub-foreman on a park road crew in 1896, made this observation which he recalled later in 1956:

> *The soldier on duty had warned him once. Even a second time the soldier asked him to desist. The third time, he collared the Englishman and started for the guardhouse. "I'll say old boy, you can't do this to me," objected the Englishman, "I'm a Count, I'm a Count." "I don't give a damn," said the soldier, "you only count one here."*

*Soldiers stationed in
Yellowstone Park, circa
1911.* Courtesy National Park
Service, Yellowstone National Park.

*Man and soldier on cone
of Old Faithful geyser,
1889.* Courtesy National Park
Service, Yellowstone National Park.

View of Fort Yellowstone from Capital Hill, early 1900s.
Courtesy National Park Service, Yellowstone National Park.

Violators of park regulations were arrested and, in some cases, escorted out of the park and denied the opportunity to re-enter.

The Army's methods of enforcing rules and regulations were often attacked by area newspapers. In defense, Captain Harris explained his administration like this:

> *In the exercise of authority which is devolved upon the office of the Superintendent of this National Park, great care has been taken to keep strictly within the limits sanctioned by law and to avoid all appearance of harsh and arbitrary exercise of authority. No person has ever been expelled from the Park who had not admitted the commission of the offense for which the penalty was enforced; and whenever there has been reason to believe that the offenses were committed without intention or through thoughtlessness, or when a sincere regret was received, the persons have been permitted to go unmolested, after suitable instruction and admonition.*

Captain Moses Harris, 1888

When the Army's administration and protection assignment in Yellowstone extended beyond temporary duty, permanent facilities were built to house the troops. The stone and wood buildings of Fort Yellowstone replaced the tent cabins of Camp Sheridan in 1891.

Soldiers considered Fort Yellowstone, built on the edge of the old Mammoth Hot Spring terraces, as a comfortable place with pleasant surroundings, relaxed discipline, and good facilities.

> [The soldiers were dressed] *in a very slovenly uniform, dark-blue blouse, and light-blue trousers unstrapped, cut spoon-shape over the boot; cartridge belt, revolver, peaked cap and worsted gloves – Black buttons!*
>
> *"And how do things go?"* [Kipling asked the soldiers.] *"Very much as you please," said they. "There's not half the discipline here that there is in the Queen's service...nor the work either, but what there is, is rough work... Our punishments? Fines mostly, and then if you carry on too much you go to the cooler – that's the clink... Horses? Oh, they're devils, these Montana horses. Bronchos mostly... Yes, they poach here. Men come in with an outfit and ponies, smuggle in a gun or two, and shoot the bison. If you interfere, they shoot at you.*

Rudyard Kipling, 1889

Army machine gun platoon drilling in front of the National Hotel at Mammoth Hot Springs, 1911. Courtesy National Park Service, Yellowstone National Park.

Interior view of the Fort Yellowstone Post Exchange, about 1900.

Courtesy National Park Service, Yellowstone National Park.

Over the years, the all-blue uniform was replaced by the blue blouse and khaki breeches of the Spanish-American War period and then eventually by an olive drab uniform with a high collared blouse, wrap-around leggings, and campaign hat.

A soldier's duty time was spent patrolling, drilling or working in the fire brigade combating forest fires in Yellowstone.

During off-duty hours soldiers read, wrote letters, fished, swam, enjoyed picnics and carriage rides, or played pool and baseball.

The Post Exchange offered a gymnasium, the sale of sundries, beer, and a place to play cards. Moving pictures were shown once a week as early as 1903. There also were religious services and occasional dances.

Our music was the finest... On one occasion we had the ladies' orchestra from Butte, Mont[ana]. We also had the Boy Band from the same place. At other times our troop soldiers furnished whatever music was needed. We have some very fine talent in the troop... Our officers at different times added to the enjoyment of the occasion by appearing with their wives.

Pvt. William H. Walsh
Soldier at Fort Yellowstone, 1895

Soldier jumping a horse during drills on the Fort Yellowstone parade grounds. Note the encouragement he is receiving from the onlookers.

Park Service, Yellowstone National Park

During the summer season, the "swaddies" (soldiers) competed against the "savages" (stagecoach drivers) for "rotten-logging" (romantic) opportunities with the young ladies employed by the hotel company.

All in all, during its thirty year assignment, the Army did a good job administering and protecting Yellowstone. Regulations were established and posted throughout the park. Patrols enforced these regulations, and the destructive trend that could have destroyed .Yellowstone was stopped. The practice of explaining the park's natural features to visitors was started, thereby making a visit to Yellowstone National Park an educational experience.

Roads, bridges, and waterworks were built. Communication between major "developed" areas of the park was improved by the stringing of telephone wires.

But a growing national park system and an increased demand to have national parks administered by a civilian organization led to the formation of the National Park Service in 1916.

On November 1, 1918, Fort Yellowstone was formally abandoned by the military. The Army days in Yellowstone ended.

The last Fourth of July cannon salute fired by the Army at Fort Yellowstone, July 4, 1916.
Jack Ellis Haynes photograph, courtesy National Park Service, Yellowstone National Park.

Ranger Naturalist staff at West Thumb Geyser Basin, 1931.
Courtesy National Park Service Yellowstone National Park

The National Park Service

DESPITE THE EXCELLENT administration and protection the Army gave Yellowstone National Park since 1886, there were notable drawbacks to the use of soldiers for this type of duty.

Generally, soldiers in Yellowstone were not well versed in outdoor skills, and because of their diverse responsibilities while on duty in the park they did not receive their full complement of military training.

By 1914 a growing movement toward a civilian administration of the growing national park system helped in the creation of the Yellowstone Park Detachment, a group of competent soldiers, skilled in outdoor park work who could be transferred to a civilian agency when they were needed.

In 1916, Congress established the National Park Service as a branch of the Department of Interior. Congress charged the National Park Service to

...promote and regulate the use of the...national parks, monuments and reservations [by] such means and measures as conform to the fundamental purpose of the said parks...which purpose is to conserve the scenery and the natural and historic objects and the wildlife therein and to provide for the enjoyment of the same in such a manner and by such means as will leave them unimpaired for the enjoyment of future generations.

National Park Service Act
Signed into law by
President Woodrow Wilson
August 25, 1916

The creation of the National Park Service gave rise to park rangers, protective agents who combined woodcraft skills, discipline, and confidence to do whatever was required in the exercise of their responsibilities. Several "scouts" transferred from the Yellowstone Park Detachment to become park rangers. These early park rangers made a good impression.

45

Park Ranger explaining thermal features to Yellowstone visitors, circa 1920s. Courtesy National Park Service, Yellowstone National Park.

...The National Park Service is the youngest of the governmental agencies, having been uniformed for the first time last summer, when it finally succeeded the regular army in policing our national playgrounds, yet it inherits from the scout organization upon which it was founded, traditions of veteran bravery, annals of sacrifice for game protection. Patterned somewhat after the Northwest mounted police of Canada, taking example from the Texas Rangers of the Rio Grande, but with an individuality of its own beyond the use of skis and motorcycles, the service, with the months, is taking form that promises to make it as powerful an arm of the law as either of the older bodies.

Spokane Statesman-Review
June 6, 1919

I was fishing the Yellowstone River across from Canyon Station. I had some fish of questionable length and my heart went up in my throat as I saw this Ranger riding toward me along the trail. I saw visions of fine and imprisonment, perhaps both, but the ranger spoke to me in a quiet voice, remarking something about the weather, and passed on. I remember how he looked as he went down the trail, moving easily with the swinging of his horse. There was something about his face, kindly, yet with a certain grim determination, that I have always remembered.

Dorr G. Yeager, 1929
on his first meeting with
Chief Ranger Samuel T. Woodring.

Chief Ranger Samuel T. Woodring, Mammoth Hot Springs, 1922.
Courtesy National Park Service, Yellowstone National Park.

Many young men applied for park ranger positions with no real idea of what the job entailed. By the end of the 1920s, Yellowstone's Superintendent began cautioning applicants.

It has been our experience that young men often apply for a place on the park ranger force with the impression or understanding that the ranger has a sort of sinecure with nothing resembling hard work to perform, and that a ranger's position offers an opportunity to pass a pleasant vacation amid the beauties and wonders of Yellowstone Park, with very frequent trips about the park and innumerable dances and other diversions to occupy one's leisure hours... with the feeling that the duties of the place require no special training or experience and that any man with a reasonably good education can perform these duties regardless of whether he has a pleasing or poor personality or whether he has or has not the experience in outdoor activities.

Roger W. Toll
Superintendent
Yellowstone National Park, 1929-1936

In truth, the work of a ranger was anything but glamorous. From the time he arose ("6:00 A.M.") until he retired ("not later than 11:00 P.M."), a Yellowstone ranger might patrol about the park either on foot or on horseback, provide information to park visitors at ranger stations, fight forest fires, explain the wonders of Yellowstone to groups of visitors, answer the same questions as if he had never heard them before ("What time does Old Faithful go off?" and "Where are the bathrooms?"), administer first aid, rescue visitors, identify flowers, cut firewood, protect the wildlife, maintain and repair trails and bridges, and complete the paperwork that each situation required.

All of this was expected for a salary of $140.00 per month, from which the ranger paid for his transportation to Yellowstone, bought his uniform ($75.00), and paid for his quarters ($5.00 per month) and meals ($1.20 per day).

Sometimes a ranger's work put him into interesting situations. A stint on road patrol could be exciting, especially when chasing speeding motorists. The narrow, winding, gravel-covered roads forced rangers to depend on guts and driving skills to catch violators. Patrol vehicles were six motorcycles and, after 1936, four V-8 Ford cars. Being thrown off motorcycles or skidding around turns in the cars was all part of the fun.

Ranger Replogle on motorcycle, 1932. Courtesy National Park Service, Yellowstone National Park

Rangers in front of Canyon Ranger Station, 1922.

Courtesy National Park Service, Yellowstone National Park.

Dan Spencer, Union Pacific Railroad advertising agent, talking with Yellowstone Park Superintendent Horace M. Albright, about 1915. Castle Geyser in background.

Courtesy Union Pacific Railroad

Apparently some impression was made on park speeders though. One wrote to the U.S. Commissioner in Mammoth Hot Springs who had fined him.

Perhaps it is not the custom for persons sentenced in your court to write and thank you for it but the whole occasion was so unusual that I cannot but do it. In the first place, I appreciated your advice thoroughly on the subject of speeding in the Park and am quite in sympathy with what you said. In regard to the fine, I think I quite deserved it. Ever since, I have been cautioning people going Parkward that the signs regarding 45 miles per hour should be read with great care and heeded equally well.

The high point for us in the whole affair was making the acquaintance of the Ranger, Lee Coleman. He drove me down from the Ranger Station and back

again and I don't think I have spent as enjoyable a day in recent years... he regaled me with the natural history of the Park in all its forms; geologically, the fauna, the flora, Indian lore, a myriad of subjects and he was remarkably well informed.

L. R. Kirk in a letter to
U.S. Commissioner T. Paul Wilcox
August 23, 1937

Then there was the operation of the bear feeding grounds. For many years, bear feeding was a visitor attraction in Yellowstone. Visitors gathered outside a fenced off arena in the evening and watched bears foraging through piles of garbage while rangers explained the bear's behavior.

Bear feeding ampitheater at Otter Creek, circa 1920s.
Courtesy National Park Service, Yellowstone National Park.

Some rangers were mortally afraid of bears and tried to cover their fears by "stuffin' dudes" (fooling tourists) with fictional adventures. One seasonal ranger's stories got so completely out of control that something had to be done. A fellow ranger tried to provide a cure

He was always coming up with these weird stories about a grizzly attacking him while he was coming home [from courting a girl at the lodge, across the river from the ranger station]... *and I said, "Well, I'll give that fellow something to talk about," so one evening I took a pair of whooly chaps, that I used to ride in when it was cold, and walked over to Chittenden Bridge. I got down right by the edge and kneeled there for a long time, until I heard him coming. I reared up and wrapped those wooly chaps over his head and you never heard such an unGodly scream out of a man as he lit out for the ranger station.*

Edward E. "Ted" Ogston
From his personal recollections as a
Yellowstone Park Ranger in the 1920s

Apparently, the cure didn't work because the young ranger used his frightening experience to develop yet another tall tale.

During the off-season, the rangers managed the elk and bison in the park. By keeping them within the park, the rangers hoped to prevent large losses of animals through hunting and starvation.

A bison ranch was maintained in the Lamar River valley where a sizeable herd was fed, innoculated, and periodically culled.

As an offshoot of this game management, rangers also engaged in predator control. Coyotes, wolves, and cougars were considered detrimental to the ungulate herds, and hundreds were trapped, shot, or poisoned each year until these practices were prohibited in 1934.

Bison Ranch operations were headquartered in the Lamar River valley until 1954.
Courtesy National Park Service, Yellowstone National Park.

Another off-season ranger activity was the border patrol, a duty carried over from the Army scout days as part of the constant campaign against poachers. Daily patrols by Yellowstone rangers, based out of isolated backcountry cabins, had all the potential, just as with the Army scouts before them, for creating lonely experiences.

But many early Yellowstone rangers considered this to be rangering reduced to its simplest and best terms. They had a good life, and it wasn't without sadness that they left when retirement forced them out of the park and the job they loved so well.

One ranger left a simple but eloquent note in his patrol cabin after he finished the last day of thirty-four years of service.

They won't let me sleep in their cabins any more.

Harry Trischman
Assistant Chief Ranger
December 31, 1945

54

Assistant Chief Ranger Harry Trischman, 1930. Courtesy National Park Service, Yellowstone National Park.

Co. R. E. Gardiner, early Yellowstone Park visitor, 1877.
Courtesy National Park Service, Yellowstone National Park.

Touring Yellowstone

SOON AFTER THE Yellowstone wilderness became Yellowstone National Park in 1872, tourists began visiting the park to enjoy themselves and to see the natural features protected here.

The first Yellowstone tourists were rugged frontier people, accustomed to roughing it and providing for themselves. Since there were only a few, very crude, overnight accommodations available in the Park, these early tourists brought everything they needed to cope with the Yellowstone wilderness with them.

As more and more tourists visited Yellowstone, concession businesses developed to meet the growing needs of these visitors.

The railroads became interested in the growing Yellowstone tourist business and built spur lines closer to the Park's entrances. They offered a trip to Yellowstone National Park as an attractive option to their regular schedules.

In the early years, most Yellowstone tourists arrived via the Northern Pacific Railroad. They traveled from the eastern or western portions of the country on the main transcontinental route and then changed to the Yellowstone Park branch line in Livingston, Montana.

[Livingston, Montana is] *a town of 2,000 people and a junction for the little sideline that takes you to the Yellowstone National Park... There is one street in the town where the cowboy's pony, and the little foal of the brood mare in the buggy, rest contentedly in the blinding sunshine while the cowboy gets himself shaved at the only barber shop and swaps lies at the bar.*

Rudyard Kipling, 1889

Northern Pacific passenger train arriving at the Gardiner, Montana, depot, 1904. For years Gardiner was the major visitor entrance to the Park.

Courtesy National Park Service, Yellowstone National Park.

Six-horse tally-ho stagecoach loaded with park visitors leaving the Gardiner depot bound for the National Hotel in Mammoth Hot Springs, 1904.

Courtesy National Park Service, Yellowstone National Park.

58

By 1903, the Northern Pacific Railroad had extended its spur line to Gardiner, Montana, Yellowstone's north entrance and for years the major visitor gateway to the park. Package tours of Yellowstone National Park were sold to railroad patrons.

Most visitors boarded six-horse, tally-ho stagecoaches at the Gardiner depot for the five mile trip up the hill to the National Hotel in Mammoth Hot Springs.

The National Hotel at Mammoth Hot Springs has a large veranda running the full length of the front. Green with a red roof, it is a most imposing structure. It is heated by several large stoves, each room has an electric call bell and the public areas are lighted by electric arc lights. There is a museum, a bar, a barber shop, several parlors for ladies and gentlemen, a news stand, and a kitchen range that can accommodate 15 cooks and feed 5,000 tourists.

Anonymous

There was also a picture shop at Mammoth Hot Springs run by F. Jay Haynes, the official photographer for Yellowstone National Park.

Haynes first visited Yellowstone in 1881 and found here a source of images which fascinated him for the rest of his life. He created thousands of "views" of Yellowstone's wonders, park "improvements," and the dressed-up Victorian era visitors who enjoyed them.

Six-horse tally-ho stagecoach arriving at the National Hotel in Mammoth Hot Springs, 1904. These stagecoaches were used to transport park visitors from the rail depot in Gardiner to the hotel in Mammoth. Later they boarded smaller stagecoaches or private buggies for their tour of Yellowstone. Courtesy National Park Service, Yellowstone National Park.

Haynes established a summer residence and studio at Mammoth Hot Springs and sold his "views" to early park visitors. His shop later expanded throughout the park, and his "views" were sold nationwide through mail order catalogs and retail outlets.

In 1916, Jack Ellis Haynes took over the business and followed in his father's footsteps as a professional photographer in Yellowstone. Some of their images are featured here in *Old Yellowstone Views.*

During their stay in the Mammoth area, these early Yellowstone visitors had the opportunity to watch the U.S. Army carry out its role of administering and protecting Yellowstone National Park.

During our stay in Mammoth, we witnessed the soldiers at drill on the parade ground in front of the hotel. On our walk about the terraces the soldier who escorted us was polite but would not permit us to carry away a bit of the formations.

Anonymous

Stagecoach in front of National Hotel, Mammoth Hot Springs.
Courtesy of National Park Service, Yellowstone National Park.

The next day, Yellowstone visitors boarded smaller stagecoaches or rented private buggies and began their tour of Yellowstone National Park.

Stagecoach tours included stops at all the scenic attractions *plus* dust, rain, mosquitos, mud, and the possibility of bandits, Indian attack, or runaway horses. Dressed in linen dusters or dime store western outfits, most Yellowstone tourists thought the adventures were worth the discomforts.

Late in the night we ran over a skunk... Everything that has been said about the skunk is true. It is an Awesome Stink.

Rudyard Kipling, 1889

Continual gymnastics are required to keep the coach upright on slopes which often exceed 45 degrees, both vertically and lengthways. Unless the driver and the travelers are always on the footboards in order to stabilize the vehicle, it would fall a hundred times a day to the bottom of steep ravines, or would be carried away by river currents... [River] crossings are very hazardous, we take all necessary precautions, in order, should there be an accident, to save the things most necessary to us; our compass, our maps, and the barrel of brandy.

Auguste Sequin, 1879

62

Stagecoaches and wagons on the Corkscrew Road near Sylvan Pass, East Entrance Road, 1910.
Courtesy National Park Service, Yellowstone National Park.

John Yancy and his dog.
Courtesy National Park Service, Yellowstone National Park.

Large hotels catered to the lodging needs of Yellowstone's visitors. There were several hotels throughout Yellowstone, each one built approximately one day's travel by stagecoach from the next. Crude as they seemed by European standards, they were welcome havens at the end of a day's rough ride.

In between the hotels were various "rest stops," lunch stations, and smaller way-side hotels. These establishments provided a chance for tourists to stretch their legs, get something to eat, and meet some of Yellowstone's more colorful characters.

Larry Matthews, the manager and genial host of the Norris Lunch Station, was the incomparable king of making tired, dusty, hungry tourists feel right at home.

Larry enveloped us all in the golden glamor of his speech ere we had descended and the tent with the rude trestle table became a palace, the rough fare delicacies of Delmonico's, and we, the abashed recipients of Larry's imperial bounty.

Rudyard Kipling, 1889

"Uncle John" Yancy's way-station on the Mammoth-Cooke City road was another favorite stopping place. "Uncle John," like Larry Matthews, was one of the Yellowstone characters that tourists looked forward to meeting.

Buggy on the road underneath Overhanging Cliff, near Tower Fall, 1913
Courtesy National Park Service, Yellowstone National Park

64

Yancy was of that frontier type which is no more to be seen; the goat-bearded, shrewd-eyed, lank Uncle Sam type. He and his cabins had been there a long while... He was known as Uncle John by that whole country.

Owen Wister, 1887

Another diversion from the regular "Grand Tour" was the opportunity to sail aboard the steamboat that plied the waters of Yellowstone Lake.

Steamboat service on the lake began in the summer of 1889 when E.C. Waters, head of the Yellowstone Lake Boat Company, hauled into Yellowstone the 40 ton steel hull of the steamer *Zillah*.

The *Zillah* measured eighty-one feet in length, fourteen feet at the beam, and could carry 120 passengers between the stagecoach lunch station at Thumb Bay and the Lake Hotel, with a stop at the animal enclosure on Dot Island.

The steamer Zillah *on Yellowstone Lake.*
Courtesy National Park Service, Yellowstone National Park.

65

The steamer E. C. Waters on Yellowstone Lake. This was a publicity photograph of the new steamboat which never sailed with passengers aboard.

Courtesy National Park Service, Yellowstone National Park.

In 1905, using materials hauled in by horse and wagon, a wooden steamer 125 feet in length and 26 feet at the beam was constructed on the shores of Yellowstone Lake. This vessel was thought adequate to transport 500 passengers, and, in anticipation of increased profits, she was christened the *E.C. Waters* after her owner.

Success was elusive, however, for the authorities refused to license the *E.C. Waters* for her requested number of passengers, suggesting instead a capacity of 125.

Mr. Waters refused to compromise. He anchored his new steamer on the east side of Stevenson Island where it remained for sixteen years.

In 1921, ice from the lake's spring thaw blew toward the island pushing the steamer onto the beach where it remained. In 1926 the machinery was removed and used to heat the Lake Hotel. Later the hulk was burned. The *E.C. Waters* never sailed with passengers aboard.

Waitresses at the National Hotel, Mammoth Hot Springs, 1925.

Courtesy National Park Service, Yellowstone National Park.

Old Faithful Inn, about 1925.
Courtesy National Park Service,
Yellowstone National Park.

Stagecoaches in front of the Canyon Hotel, about 1913.
Courtesy National park Service, Yellowstone National Park.

Park visitors climbing in the Grand Canyon of the Yellowstone, 1904.
Courtesy National Park Service, Yellowstone National Park.

Because of the travel expense involved, Yellowstone National Park was patronized at first primarily by the wealthy "carriage trade," those persons who normally spent the summer gadabouting in Europe. In keeping with the unspoken social rules of the day, most photographs show these visitors in somber, starched collar poses with the required calm demeanor.

"Permanent Camps," or "tent hotels," sprung up for those Yellowstone visitors desiring cheaper accommodations. These camps were located a day's travel apart and featured brightly colored candy-striped tents and informal campfire programs. They were very popular.

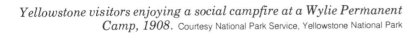

Yellowstone visitors enjoying a social campfire at a Wylie Permanent Camp, 1908. Courtesy National Park Service, Yellowstone National Park

69

A Wylie Permanent Camp, prior to 1915.
Courtesy National Park Service, Yellowstone National Park.

A tent hotel, sometimes called a "krawl" is something fearful and wonderful; there appears to be a fixed price for every item – one dollar... The "Grub Pile" [food] does not differ much at different meals, and if the traveler wants to know what meal is set before him, consultation with the host or the watch is requisite... As for furniture, the tent is not so bad; an ingenius adaptation in iron of the earthen stove, used from time immemorial by Indians, keeps the frost out, a pine stump or two stick up conveniently out of the ground, beds [are] of considerable capacity, well furnished with blankets... During the height of the season the principle upon which the beds are populated is said to be the addition of visitors so long as they may arrive, or until the occupants "go for their guns." The plan is simple, and relieves the authorities of responsibility.

Thomas Henry Thomas, 1886

Interior of a Wylie Permanent Camp dining tent, 1912.
Courtesy National Park Service, Yellowstone National Park.

*Wylie Permanent
Camp maids,
about 1908.*
Courtesy National Park Service,
Yellowstone National Park.

These permanent camps and tent hotels were staffed by college students and school teachers, which may have added to the charm that some visitors found there.

> *... we came to a wooden shanty called an hotel, in time for a crazy tiffin served by very gorgeous handmaids with very pink cheeks. When health fails in other and more exciting pursuits, a season as "help" in one of the Yellowstone hotels will restore the frailest constitution.*

Rudyard Kipling, 1889

*Lake Hotel
employees, 1904.*
Courtesy National Park Service,
Yellowstone National Park.

Visitors wading in water of Great Fountain Geyser.

[The boy]must have been somewhere in his 'teens; he was like the true love in "Twelfth Night" that could sing both high and low. In calm moments he would answer you in a deep bass. In excitement, into which he periodically fell, the bass cracked to a wild treble... We would be sitting tilted back, reading our mail, the tourists would have ceased talking and be lounging drowsily, the boy would be at the door, motionless as a steel trap. Suddenly, the trap would spring, the boy would catapult into the door, and in his piping treble scream out: "Beehive's a-goin' off!" at which every tourist instantly started from his chair, and a leaping crowd gushed out of the hotel and sprinted down over the formation to catch Beehive at it. Beehive finally quiescent, they returned slowly, sank into their chairs and exhausted silence; you could have heard a mosquito. But the steel trap was again set, sprang soon, and again the silence was pierced: "There goes Old Faithful!"

Up and out they flew once more, watched Old Faithful, and came back to their chairs and to silence more exhausted.

Was the boy exhausted? Never. It might be the Castle, it might be Grotto – whatever it might be, that [boy] routed those torpid tourists from their repose to set them trooping across the formation to gape at some geyser in action, and again seek their chairs, feebler each time.

Owen Wister, 1887

Park guides, 1924.
Courtesy National Park Service,
Yellowstone National Park

A couple of cowboys – real cowboys, not the Buffalo Bill article – jingled through the camp... I know that they never washed. But they were picturesque ruffians with long spurs, hooded stirrups, slouch hats, fur weather-clothes over their knees, and pistol butts easy to hand.

        Rudyard Kipling, 1889

74

Wylie Permanent Camp tent, about 1908.
Courtesy National Park Service, Yellowstone National Park.

Lake Hotel employees with fishing success.
Courtesy National Park Service, Yellowstone National Park.

Tourists on porch of National Hotel.
Courtesy National Park Service, Yellowstone National Park.

Employees at waterfall, 1904.
Courtesy National Park Service, Yellowstone National Park.

Lake Hotel with stages loading.
Courtesy National Park Service, Yellowstone National Park.

Ronald V. Nixon, 14 year old telegraph operator, National Hotel, 1925. Courtesy National Park Service, Yellowstone National Park.

Porter, Mammoth Hotel, circa 1925.
Courtesy National Park Service, Yellowstone National Park.

Bus boy, 1925. Courtesy National Park Service, Yellowstone National Park.

Touring cars entering Yellowstone National Park through the North Entrance or Roosevelt Arch. This gateway arch at Gardiner, Montana was dedicated by President Theodore Roosevelt on April 24, 1903. Courtesy National Park Service, Yellowstone National Park

In 1915, Yellowstone National Park was officially opened to the automobile. But it was not until 1917 that touring cars replaced the 600 stagecoaches and 3,000 horses as the chief form of transportation in the park.

With the admission of private automobiles, Yellowstone was accessible to anyone who could afford one and was willing to contend with the rough, winding, and rut-filled roads.

We started out from the park this morning. I never seen such grades in all my life. Steep as a barn roof. Burned out my foot-brake right off and then, by gosh, we wore out the emergency brake, too. Had to pull over to the roadside and put in new brake shoes. We was lucky to have 'em along, else we'd be stranded up there yet.

Frederic F. Van De Water, 1927

Drove through North Entrance. Had auto checked by the Ranger who set down some strict requirements. Vehicles can leave Gardiner between 6 and 6:30 AM –
no earlier, no later. Vehicles can arrive in Mammoth between 6:20 and 7:00 AM only. They can leave Mammoth between 6:45 and 7:15 AM arriving at Norris Junction between 8:30 and 9:00 and so on throughout the park. Arriving at a given point ahead of schedule makes one subject to a fine of 50 cents per minute for the first five minutes, $1.00 per minute for the next 20 minutes. Arriving anywhere 25 minutes ahead of schedule gets one fined $25.00 and ejected from the park. We had to set our watches with the Ranger at the entrance station so there would be no question as to the correct time.

Anonymous

Larry Matthews on the porch of his lunch station at Norris Geyser Basin, 1904.
Courtesy National Park Service, Yellowstone National Park.

North Entrance automobile checking station, about 1923.
Courtesy National Park Service, Yellowstone National park.

Automobile stuck in the muddy, rut-filled road through Yellowstone's Hayden Valley.

Yellowstone National Park became the goal of many American motorists. A new type of visitor came to Yellowstone and was encouraged to camp along the roadsides. Because they generally did just that, these visitors were known as "sagebrushers."

A system of free automobile campgrounds has been developed and many of these are available for use during the season... These campgrounds accommodate hundreds of cars. For the motorist who does not care to camp in the extensive campgrounds at the many points of interest, smaller camp sites, easily recognized by signs such as "Good Camp," with pure water and wood for cooking, have been designated.

From a 1932 National Park
Service brochure describing
Yellowstone National Park

Sagebrusher automobile camp, 1923. Courtesy National Park Service, Yellowstone National Park.

WHAT TO WEAR

Warm clothing should be worn and one should be prepared for the sudden changes of temperature common at an altitude of 7,500 feet. [Travelers] should have medium-weight overcoats and sweaters. Linen dusters are desirable. Stout shoes should be worn, as they are best suited for walking about the geysers and terraces and for mountain use. Knickers are very sensible garments for those energetic persons who like to climb, ride or tramp. Tinted glasses and serviceable gloves should be part of the traveler's outfit and a pair of field glasses will be found useful.

From a Northern Pacific Railroad
Advertising brochure regarding
Yellowstone National Park.

For those who preferred to leave the driving to someone else, there were guided trips aboard "luxurious" touring cars. Large parades of these vehicles departed from the various hotels daily and strung out along the roads of Yellowstone. Despite the wind and the dust, visitors delighted in the experience of traveling forty-five miles-per-hour.

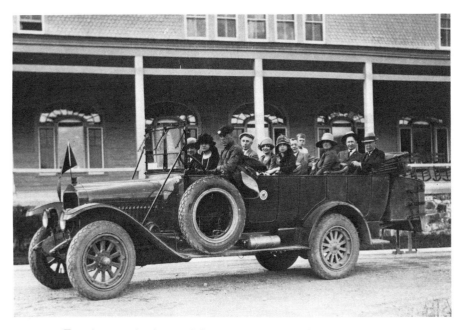

Touring car in front of the Mammoth Hot Springs Hotel, 1925. Yellowstone Park Superintendent Horace M. Albright is seated in rear.

Courtesy National Park Service, Yellowstone National Park.

Automobile campers, 1924. Courtesy National Park Service, Yellowstone National Park.

Visitors at Grotto Geyser.

Courtesy National Park Service, Yellowstone National Park.

At brink of Upper Falls.

Courtesy National Park Service, Yellowstone National Park.

At a hot spring, 1904.

Courtesy National Park Service, Yellowstone National Park.

At Handkerchief Pool, 1904.

Courtesy National Park Service, Yellowstone National Park.

Coast to coast in a flivver. Two young men pose with their automobile while visiting Yellowstone National Park in 1922. Courtesy National Park Service, Yellowstone National Park.

Early motorhome in Mammoth Hot Springs auto camp, 1924.
Courtesy National Park Service, Yellowstone National Park.

With the advent of motorized travel throughout Yellowstone, many of the permanent camps and tent hotels and even some of the regular hotels were forced to close. The automobile eliminated the need for these intermediate accommodations.

Access to Yellowstone was democratized by the automobile which truly opened the national park "for the benefit and enjoyment of the people." Even more visitors flocked to see the park, and Yellowstone entered another era.

Looking back as we have done, it is easy to see how the methods of visiting Yellowstone have changed. But the nostalgia and the excitement still linger. Despite the years, the reasons for visiting Yellowstone remain the same.

I have just completed the six days' circular journey by stage through the Yellowstone National Park. I am moved to admiration, but still more to awe.

David M. Steele, 1917

First automobile over Sylvan Pass, East Entrance road, July, 1914.

Courtesy National Park Service, Yellowstone National Park

BIBLIOGRAPHY

Yellowstone's First Visitors

Beal, Merrill D., *The Story of Man in Yellowstone,* Caldwell, Idaho: Caxton Printers, 1949.

Boesch, Mark, *John Colter,* New York: Putnam, 1935.

Bonney, Orrin H., *Battle Drums and Geysers; The Life and Journals of Lt. Gustavus Cheyney Doane, Soldier and Explorer of the Yellowstone and Snake River Regions,* Chicago: Sage Books, 1970.

Brown, Mark Herbert, *The Plainsmen of the Yellowstone; A History of the Yellowstone Basin,* New York: Putnam, 1961.

Chittenden, Hiram Martin, *The Yellowstone National Park,* Ed. Richard A. Bartlett, Norman, Oklahoma: University of Oklahoma Press, 1964.

Clary, David A., *The Place Where Hell Bubbled Up,* Washington, D. C.: Office of Publications, National Park Service, U. S. Department of the Interior, 1972.

Cook, Charles W., *The Valley of the Upper Yellowstone; An Exploration of the Headwaters of the Yellowstone River in the Year 1869, as Recorded by Charles W. Cook, David E. Folsom, and William Peterson,* Ed. Aubrey L. Haines, Norman, Oklahoma: University of Oklahoma Press, 1965.

Ferris, Warren A., *Life in the Rocky Mountains, 1830-1835,* Ed. P. C. Phillips, Denver: Old West Publishing Co., 1940.

Fitzgerald, F. Scott, *The Last Tycoon,* New York: Charles Scribner's Sons, 1941.

Folsom, David E., *The Folsom-Cook Exploration of the Upper Yellowstone in the Year 1869,* St. Paul, Minnesota: H. L. Collins Co., 1894.

Haines, Aubrey L., *The Yellowstone Story, Vol. 1 and 2,* Yellowstone National Park, Wyoming: Yellowstone Library and Museum Association in cooperation with Colorado Associated University Press, 1977.

Harris, Burton, *John Colter, His Years in the Rockies,* New York: Scribner, 1952.

Langford, Nathaniel Pitt, *Journal of the Washburn Expedition to the Yellowstone and Firehole Rivers in the Year 1870,* Lincoln, Nebraska: University of Nebraska Press, 1972.

Replogle, Wayne F., *Yellowstone's Bannock Indian Trails,* Yellowstone National Park, Wyoming: Yellowstone National Park, 1956.

United States Geological Survey, *Ferdinand Vandiveer Hayden and the Founding of the Yellowstone National Park,* Washington: U. S. Government Printing Office, 1973.

U. S. War Department, *Report of Lieutenant Gustavus C. Doane, Upon the So-Called Yellowstone Expedition of 1870,* Washington: U. S. Government Printing Office, 1875.

Victor, Frances Fuller, *The River of the West,* Hartford Connecticut: R. W. Bliss and Company, 1870.

Victor, Frances Fuller, *The River of the West,* Volume I, Missoula: Mountain Press, 1983.

Yellowstone Country. Ed. Richard Phillips, Midland, Michigan: Richard Phillips, 1977.

William Henry Jackson

Hayden, Ferdinand V., *Preliminary Report of the United States Geological Survey of Adjacent Territories ...For the Year 1872,* Washington, D. C.: Government Printing Office, 1872.

Jackson, Clarence S., *Picture Maker of the Old West, William H. Jackson,* New York: Charles Scribner's Sons, 1947.

Army Days in Yellowstone

Chittenden, Hiram Martin, *The Yellowstone National Park,* Ed. Richard A. Bartlett, Norman, Oklahoma: University of Oklahoma Press, 1964.

Haines, Aubrey L., *The Yellowstone Story,Vol. 1 and 2,* Yellowstone National Park, Wyoming: Yellowstone Library and Museum Association in cooperation with Colorado Associated University Press, 1977.

Harris, Captain Moses, *Report of the Superintendent of the Yellowstone National Park to the Secretary of the Interior, 1886 and 1888,* Washington, D. C.: Government Printing Office, 1886 and 1888.

Kipling, Rudyard, *From Sea to Sea,* Garden City, New York: Doubleday, Page and Company, 1920.

Old Yellowstone Days, Ed. Paul Schullery, Boulder: Colorado Associated University Press, 1979.

Remington, Frederic, "Policing the Yellowstone," *Pony Tracks,* New York: Harper, 1898.

Walsh, W. H., "Bath's Soldier Boy," *Bath Independent,* Dec. 1895.

Wasden, James B., "Lovell Man Recalls Early-Days Work on Yellowstone Park Roads," *Billings Gazette,* 1956. Yellowstone National Park Reference Library clipping file.

Wister, Owen, "Old Yellowstone Days," *Harpers' Monthly Magazine,* March 1936.

National Park Service

Albright, Horace Marden, "Oh, Ranger!," Stanford University, California: Stanford University Press, 1928.

Carter, Forest L., *Reminiscences of an old Yellowstone Ranger Between the Years 1921 and 1926,* Grand Marais, Michigan: Grand Sable Publishing Co., 1974.

Connery, Thomas M., "The Winter Tragedy of the Yellowstone," *Wide World Magazine,* June 1919.

Haines, Aubrey L., *The Yellowstone Story, Vol. 1 and 2,* Yellowstone National Park, Wyoming: Yellowstone Library and Museum Association in cooperation with Colorado Associated University Press, 1977.

Ogston, Edward E. "Ted," From Interview at Aspen Creek, Wyoming, June 20, 1966, Yellowstone National Park Archives.

Toll, Roger W., Form Letter, Yellowstone National Park Archives, undated.

Trishman, Harry, Note left in Crevice Ranger Station, December 1945.

Yeager, Dorr G., "Some Old Timers of the Yellowstone," Typescript, Yellowstone National Park Reference Library.

Touring Yellowstone

Dunraven, Windham Thomas Wyndham-Quin, 4th Earl of, *The Great Divide: Travels in the Upper Yellowstone in the Summer of 1874,* London: Chatto and Windhus, 1876.

Haines, Aubrey L., *The Yellowstone Story, Vol. 1 and 2,* Yellowstone National Park, Wyoming: Yellowstone Library and Museum Association in cooperation with Colodado Associated University Press, 1977.

Haynes, Frank Jay, *The Yellowstone National Park,* 1900.

Haynes, Jack Ellis, *Yellowstone Stage Holdups,* Bozeman, Montana: Haynes Studios, Inc., 1959.

Haynes, Jack Ellis, *Haynes Road Log of Yellowstone National Park,* St. Paul, Minnesota: Haynes Picture Shops, 1936.

Kipling, Rudyard, *From Sea to Sea,* Garden City, New York: Doubleday, Page and Company, 1920.

National Park Service, *Circular of General Information Regarding Yellowstone National Park, Wyoming,* Washington D. C.: U. S. Government Printing Office, 1932.

Old Yellowstone Days, Ed. Paul Schullery, Boulder: Colorado Associated University Press, 1979.

Sequin, Auguste, *Ten Days on the Headwaters of the Missouri,* From an account of a trip in 1879. Manuscript in possession of Lee Whittlesey, Yellowstone National Park, translated from the original French by Chris MacIntosh.

Shaw and Powell Camping Company, *Yellowstone Park by Camp,* Livingston, Montana, undated.

Thomas, Thomas Henry, "Yellowstone Park Illustrated," *The Graphic,* August 11, 1888.

Van De Water, Frederic F., *The Family Fliver to Frisco,* New York: D. Appleton and Co., 1927.

Wister, Owen, "Old Yellowstone Days," *Harper's Monthly Magazine,* March, 1936.

Wylie Permanent Camping Co., *Yellowstone National Park,* Livingston, Montana, 1912-1913.